THE LANDSCAPES OF OUR PATIENTS' JOURNEYS

By Keith A. Rasey, M. Div., LNHA Chaplain

Copyright 2011 Keith A. Rasey

Published by Phoenix Press
908 Laurel Glens Dr.
Medina, OH 44256

All rights reserved

TABLE OF CONTENTS

Acknowledgements
Foreword
Introduction
Chapter One: Preparing to Join the Journey
Chapter Two: Surveying the Landscapes
Chapter Three: The Landscape of Fear
Chapter Four: The Landscape of Death Avoidance
Chapter Five: The Landscape of Neutral Acceptance
Chapter Six: The Landscape of Approach Acceptance
Chapter Seven: The Landscape of Escape Acceptance
Chapter Eight: The Variegated Landscape: All Over the Place
Endnotes
Bibliography

ACKNOWLEDGEMENTS

I owe a great debt to many people. Jeanne Bennett, teacher of the adult development class at Kent, piqued my interest in the ways people face the final wave aka death. Sue McCausland urged me to submit a proposal for the workshop out of which this book grew. Jennifer Cleric was kind enough to review most of the content. Father Ed Luca was very kind to loan me two hymnal/service books from the Roman Catholic tradition. Michelle Vancisin, my daughter, a published author in her own right, helped me with putting it in a format that was useable by ebooks.

Diane Davies Rasey, my wife, was kind enough to read the manuscript and offer suggestions on how to sharpen it.

Of course, any mistakes in the book are completely my own responsibility as, to quote, the Psalmist, "my sins are ever before me." Please contact me to report errors or formatting issues at krasey1@kent.edu .

Although I wanted to do a more expansive work that included resources from all the major religions, it soon became apparent that would be unworkable. I hope this will be useful to those who accompany patients and their loved ones at the end of their lives here.

Keith A. Rasey, M. Div, LNHA
Medina, Ohio 2011

FOREWORD

It has only been a short time that I have had the privilege to work with Keith Rasey in hospice care. We have had the opportunity to work together in building a new hospice program from the ground up. During this time, I have come to know him as deeply thoughtful, highly intelligent, and fiercely passionate about hospice care. He obtained his Master of Divinity degree from Yale University and has led a number of Christian congregations. He has been a pioneer in the hospice movement, having provided pastoral care to the very first hospice patient in the United States in 1977. While he has done various types of work in his lifetime, his calling has always been the care of the dying.

This book itself has been an intense challenge as well as a labor of love. Because of his commitment as a spiritual counselor in hospice care, Keith has found the writing and creative process to also be an evolution in his career as well as a time of growth in his perception of self.

In the time that I have been working alongside Keith, I have been convinced of the power found in relating to each individual's narrative during end of life care, and the importance of relating to them within that context. As caregivers we are always striving to improve our practice and do better by our patients and families. Herein is a powerful reminder that for all our knowledge and expertise, we have the opportunity to not only provide silent witness or passive presence, but allow the patient to guide us on their journey. We can bear witness on this journey to the grave spiritual concerns they face at end of life, and with insight we may have permission to provide individualized spiritual care.

This book provides a construct in which the patient 'journeys through a landscape' as a metaphor for the emotional and spiritual experiences we witness at the end of life. The skilled nature of our care as professionals compels us to search for a way to individualize our response to spiritual distress or pain. This construct allows for just that. Rasey shows us how the use of a data collection tool that helps identify the domain or 'landscape' in which the patient finds themselves can help us individualize spiritual care. He shows us how we can come alongside the patient in presence, but also helping them identify landmarks in the landscape. In other words, we can learn how to journey with the patient and help them identify issues or concerns they need to address, instead of imposing a cookie cutter solution of what we think might help.

Most importantly, it is about the patient's journey. Not our response to it. The patient remains the center of care. And the better we are able to assess and develop insight about the landscape through which they travel, the more focused and effective our care can be.

    Jennifer Cleric RN, ND
    Aurora, Ohio 2011

INTRODUCTION

The variety of landscapes our patients journey through is breathtaking. Some are mountainous. Some are plains. Some are valleys.

Some are lush and can nurture all kinds of life. Some are arid and it is difficult for any living creature to survive.

Some are stony with monochromatic colors and themes. Some are full of beautiful flowers that make the journey pleasant.

Some landscapes are a combination of many different kinds of terrain and flora and fauna that change with the seasons.

The landscapes can change from day to day, sometimes even hour to hour, minute to minute.

If we listen to our patients and their loved ones, we can discern the contours of the landscapes through which they are traveling. The words, metaphors, symbols and imagery they use will unfold their landscapes for us. The often asked question of end of life caregivers, "What do you say to someone who is dying?" is answered by a deep listening in which we use the language of the patients'/families' own landscapes to let them know we are listening, we are present.

We do not have to search for our responses because the language, even when it is just silent witness, is given to us through the act of listening while fully present and available to them. They are not alone.

We help validate their journeys by accompanying them. In the end, the ideal and ultimate goal of our companionship with them is to reassure them that it was worth the trip—for both them and for us.

Chapter One

Preparing to Join the Journey

Before we can effectively accompany our patients and their families through the landscapes of their journeys, we have to be sure we have all we need to be helpful and useful. The main instrument of our accompaniment will be our own beings. Who we are and how we are will determine if we can be fully present with our patients to completely hear and employ the words, symbols, metaphors and images they use to describe the landscapes they are traversing.

It was axiomatic, for example, in medieval Christian thought, that only one who was fully ready to die was capable of fully living. *Momento Mori*, "remember you will die," is one of the mantras intimately connected with contemplative prayer and spiritual formation, especially in monasticism (cf. http://inspirituetveritate.blogspot.com and the comments there about "Momento Mori and Joy"). To be aware of one's own mortality and humble "creatureliness" (See Note 1) is to realize that now is the time we have. Of the time before we were born there is no personal memory and of the time after death, there is only the hope. Now is the time to embrace life.

This may seem morbid to modern and postmodern sensibilities as we are used to the many ways in which the emphasis on progress has repressed the fact that every creature has a lifespan with a beginning and an end (See Note 2). Those who are accustomed to relating to persons who know they are going to die—and it is more imminent than most are willing to acknowledge— realize the freedom and liberation that comes from this knowledge.

But this liberation from the many cares that keep us from fully living, with the terrible knowledge of our mortality, in the glory of each moment is something that caregivers are to practice with our own attitudes and habits if we are to realize its benefits for our patients. It means we are to be fully capable of overcoming the alienation we have between our bodies and our "souls," our hearts and our minds (See Note 3).

The ability to fully hear and completely listen—with all our being—to our patients and families is the necessary prerequisite to accompanying them effectively through the landscapes of their journeys. Thus, overcoming the duality between any opposites within our own being becomes crucial. Our effectiveness as listeners, witnesses and companions requires that we become bodysouls, mindhearts, complete and whole human creatures.

> As Lao Tzu said it:
> Is there a difference between yes and no?
> Is there a difference between good and evil?
> Must I fear what others fear? What nonsense!
> Having and not having arise together
> Difficult and easy complement each other
> Long and short contrast each other
> High and low rest upon each other
> Front and back follow one another.

To those of a more philosophical bent, it may be helpful to remember what Alfred North Whitehead wrote about the unitary nature of all that is.

> "That is, all the things and events we usually consider…irreconcilable, such as cause and effect, past and future, subject and object, are actually just like the crest and trough of a single wave….For a wave, although itself a single event, only expresses itself through the opposites of crest and trough, high point

and low point. For that very reason the reality is not found in the crest nor the trough alone, but in their unity (try to imagine a wave with crests but no troughs). Obviously, there's no such thing as a crest without a trough, a high point without a low point. Crest and trough—indeed all opposites—are inseparable aspects of one underlying activity." (See Note 4).

To approach our patients and families with only our hearts or our minds is to not fully use all of the resources we have been given and developed. An approach which is all heart may be so full of sentimentality that it will not be effective. An approach which is all mind may be equally ineffective because it will seem heartless, inauthentic and hollow.

Henri Nouwen has reminded us of the resources of the Desert Fathers and Mothers for spiritual practices that can help us overcome this alienation. In *The Way of the Heart* he writes of what happens when we **think** of prayer as something we do with part of our being:

> For many of us prayer means nothing more than speaking with God. And since it usually seems to be a quite one-sided affair, prayer simply means talking to God. This idea is enough to create great frustrations. If I present a problem, I expect a solution; if I formulate a question, I expect an answer; if I ask for guidance, I expect a response. And when it seems, increasingly, that I am talking into the dark, it is not so strange that I soon begin to suspect that my dialogue with God is in fact a monologue. Then I may begin to ask myself: To whom am I really speaking, God or myself? (See Note 5).

Please note the duality of how he states this view of prayer: problem/solution, question/answer, guidance/response. Approaching our spiritual preparation—whatever we call it—as if it is separate from our personhood and our work is a formula for failure. It reinforces the alienation that prevents us from being fully present with our patients/families.

Nouwen goes on to say more about just approaching preparation with our minds:

> "But there is another viewpoint that can lead to similar frustrations. This is the viewpoint that restricts the meaning of prayer to thinking about God. Whether we call this prayer or meditation makes little difference. The basic conviction is that what is needed is to think thoughts about God and his [sic] mysteries. Prayer therefore requires hard mental work and is quite fatiguing, especially. If reflective thinking is not one of our strengths. Since we already have so many other practical and pressing things on our minds, thinking about God becomes one more demanding burden. This is especially true because thinking about God is not a spontaneous event, while thinking about pressing concerns comes quite naturally."(See Note 6).

The answer, for the Desert Fathers and Mothers, comes by entering with our minds into the sanctuary of our hearts to present all of ourselves to God. In this practice, alienation becomes swallowed up in wholeness, we are truly skilled and experienced at being body/souls, mind/hearts and can offer this wholeness (note the connection of that word to holiness) to our patients/families.

> We find the best formulation of the prayer of the heart in the words of the Russian Theophan the Recluse: "To pray is to descend with the mind into the heart, and there to stand before the face of the Lord, ever-present, all-seeing, within you." Prayer is standing in the presence of God with the mind in the heart; that is, at that point of our being where there are no divisions or

distinctions and where we are totally one. There God's Spirit dwells and there the great encounter takes place. There heart speaks to heart, because there we stand before the face of the Lord, all-seeing, within us (See Note 7).

It is not even necessary to put this in a religious context. From a psychological perspective, the ideal is to be self-differentiated—a person who is sufficiently self developed to be able to posit "I" when others are putting on the pressure to say the blaming "you" or the co-opting "we." The difference between self-differentiation and narcissism is that the self-differentiated person is still connected by relationship with others. She is not isolated but rather defines herself by her relationships, especially their quality, with others. The narcissist is too wrapped up in herself to take the time to form quality relationships of depth with others.

The caregiver who is self-differentiated will be able to be connected to the patients and families without being fused with their grief or fear or anger or terror. Without sufficient self-differentiation, one can become so fused with the issues and feelings of the patient/family that the intensity squeezes the life out of all concerned. Fusion overwhelms the caregiver and makes the caregiver ineffective. In the long run, it leads to exhaustion and burn out.

This can be illustrated by the difference between a circuit of light bulbs that is connected in series and a circuit that is connected in parallel. In the circuit that is connected in series, when one light goes out, they all go out. This is fusion—the darkness of one unit magnifies the darkness of all. The dis-ease is catching.

Those who are connected like a parallel circuit, represent precisely the opposite. When one experiences terror or grief or pain, all the others continue to shine offering, by their presence, respite and wholeness.(See Note 8).

Another way to explore fusion can be borrowed from ego psychology. The collapse of ego boundaries leads to role overfunction which may result in harm to the caregiver and the patient/family. It is commonly known, in ethical terms, what it means to violate the boundaries of a patient as far as information or privacy or unhealthy touching and sexualized attention. The goal of healthy boundaries is to prevent fusion by encouraging the caregiver to "stay in their own skin" and not be overwhelmed by the needs or concerns of the patient/family. Here it becomes necessary to know the limits of one's own boundaries so as not to assume a godlike relationship in meeting the needs of the other. This also prevents burn out by encouraging the self-care of maintaining healthy boundaries. Only a god is available all the time, 24 hours, seven days a week. The rest of us are to savor our limits and keep our boundaries inviolate in order to bring our own healthy selfhood as an instrument of healing and hope to our patients.

To overfunction in our role as caregivers and be fused is to do more for the patient than is in the best interest of the patient's maximal functioning, integrity and well being. Greater life satisfaction, and better outcomes, result when we only provide the care for the patient that the patient cannot perform for him or herself. To encourage the patient to provide as much self care and self regulation as possible is to truly help them live until they say good bye. Fusion deprives the patient of autonomy and transfers the benefits of the joys of their living more to the caregiver rather than primarily to the patient.

A helpful metaphor, by Henri Nouwen, is to think of two separate hands. If each hand has its fingers tightly intertwined with the fingers of the other, they will form a two handed fist with all the violence that can imply. They are fused—so closely intertwined they are squeezing the life out of each other. In a healthy relationship that is not fused, each hand oscillates, in a kind of relational dance, back and forth with the other. At times, the two separate hands can come together in a prayer or Namaste position which transcends the "aloneness" of each and points to the transpersonal realm of everlasting peace.

Buddhism is particularly helpful in offering a way of imagining this process of spiritual preparation/self-differentiation which is a prerequisite for effectively accompanying our patients/families on their journeys. Joan Halifax, a Zen Priest, in *Being with Dying*, reaffirms the necessity of preparing for dying in order to fully live. In fact, she notes it is one of the central tenets of Buddhist meditative practice:

> After four decades of sitting with dying people and their caregivers, I believe that studying the process of how to die well benefits even those of us who may have many years of life ahead. Yet, the sooner we can embrace death, the more time we have to live completely, and to live in reality. Our acceptance of our death influences not only the experience of dying but also the experience of living; life and death lie along the same continuum. One cannot—as so many of us try to do—lead life fully *and* struggle to keep the inevitable at bay (See Note 9).

She notes one of the helpful meditative metaphors in Buddhism is "strong back, soft front." By strong back she means the development of the practice of being rooted and grounded, through the posture of the spine, in one's own center so that one has the strength to face all that comes one's way. It would not be too misrepresentative—and I hope it is helpful— to note it helps us to unpack the meaning of this with the psychological concept of self-differentiation.

Please notice that the very way she refers to the meditative practice of "strong back, soft front" locates the strengthening of the whole person in the body. There is no separation of the body from the spirit or the temporal from the eternal. Meditative practice, in Buddhism, can be a way to be connected to the whole of the universe and all that is, was and will be. Duality and alienation are swallowed up in the practice of connecting to the "boundless abode." In this way, we are fully and timelessly present with our patients/families.

By "soft front" she refers to a comfortable posture of the body of openness to all that is, was and will be. It is a stance of practicing the connection with the boundless abode that, by the very posture of the body, indicates one is open to receiving all that is offered or can potentially be offered. The bodily stance of "soft front" can be sitting upright with your hands at your knees of folded in your lap embodying your openness to those you are with.

"Soft front" is a way of envisioning meditative practice that prepares us to let our patients/families know that we are open to receive all that they have to offer, share and experience, no matter how wonderful, or how terrible. It grounds empathy in our spiritual practice and redeems it from mere sentiment.

When combined, the practice of "strong back, soft front" makes us accessible without overwhelming us with the patients/families' concerns. It fully establishes we can accompany our patients/families anywhere in the landscape of their journey no matter how rugged or arduous. ""Strong back, soft front" makes us capable of withstanding any patient's journey and grounds our care giving in a sustainable, long lasting professional posture.

"Strong back, soft front" in its combination of the one with the All and the body with the boundless abode, overcomes alienation and prepares us to be fully and completely present as we accompany our patients and families in the landscapes of their journeys and plumb the depths of their words, metaphors, symbols and images.

No matter how we envision or approach it— entering with our minds into the sanctuaries of our hearts, self-differentiation, "strong back, soft front"— each of these ways of preparing ourselves offers us the capability of effectively accompanying our patients/families as they navigate the landscapes of their journeys. The preparation sharpens our listening skills for we bring all of our beings to the moment. The preparation sharpens our abilities to notice the landscapes we traverse and note their uniqueness as well as their commonalities. This preparation enables us to recognize the challenges and the joys of each landscape so that the trip becomes worthwhile for the patients and the families. The landscape's words, metaphors, symbols and images themselves, then, offer the nourishment we need to truly enjoy our work and thrive for the long run.

Ultimately, our preparation for being with our patients/families as they find their way through the landscapes of their journeys, not only makes us more effective, it sustains us for the long run by making it possible for us to see the gifts that the patients'/families' landscapes offer us.

Confucius was presented with a life and death conundrum. Either thread a continuous fiber through nine small holes in a gem or die. What to do? Then he overheard a small girl, near a mulberry bush, say the Chinese word for "secret" which sounds like the Chinese word for "honey." That provided the solution. He tied a thread from the mulberry bush onto an ant, dipped the gem in honey and let the ant blissfully solve the problem (See Note 10).

In all of our preparation and our companionship with our patients and families through the particular landscapes of their journeys, we can look for, and learn to recognize, the sweetness that makes all of the difficulties worthwhile. Without it, we are going through the motions. With it, we have found the nourishment in our patients' landscapes that makes their trips worthwhile and helps us look forward to the next journey, and our own, with anticipation.

Chapter Two

Surveying the Landscape
The Death Attitudes Profile-Revised

In *The Psychology of Death*, Robert Kastenbaum notes that the American health care system "prefers not to notice how people think, feel, and communicate at the point of death."(See Note 1). He does concede that hospice personnel are "often" more sensitive to the needs of the dying and their loved ones but are just as likely as other health care providers to feel the pressure to do the paperwork necessary to fulfill the regulatory requirements and provide the medical care needed.

Kastenbaum's research, using a kind of "modified psychological autopsy method," helped better understand the specifics of the context of the "personality and lifestyle, and…the circumstances and events that a person had moved through as the end approached."(See Note 2) This leads to better care and more sensitively appropriate responses and interventions. "We realized (sometimes too late) that having known the person a little better previously could have helped us offer more sensitive and appropriate care at the time that a…setting was becoming a deathbed scene" (See Note 3).

Efforts to more accurately assess the attitudes and beliefs of the dying and their loved ones are necessary, then, in order to provide the best possible care while there is still time for living, caring, laughing and loving.

There are many instruments available to assess acceptance of death and anxiety about its presence and, perhaps, imminence. The choice of the Death Attitude Profile-Revised (DAP-R) is somewhat arbitrary. It does, however, offer some advantages over other instruments. It is multidimensional, has content validity, internal consistency and is broader than many of the other instruments available.

The DAP-R, displayed at the end of this chapter, consists of 32 statements concerning attitudes toward death. The respondent is asked to rate his/her response either as Strongly Agree, Agree, Mostly Agree, Neutral, Mostly Disagree, Disagree or Strongly Disagree. Each response is evaluated by being given a number from one to seven, with one being Strongly Disagree and seven representing Strongly Agree.

The statements on the DAP-R are grouped into five dimensions, one of which will be explained in each of the succeeding five chapters (along with corresponding hymns, readings, prayer/meditation themes). For each dimension, the mean score can then be calculated by adding up the numerical value of all the responses and dividing by the statements in that dimension.

It is multidimensional in that it does not just measure death anxiety or death acceptance but these five factorially derived dimensions:

Fear of Death conceptualized as confronting death and the feelings of fear it evokes.

Death Avoidance conceptualized as avoiding all thoughts or references to death in order to reduce death anxiety.

Approach/Acceptance in which death is viewed as a gateway to a happy afterlife.

Escape Acceptance which is the view of death as escape from a painful existence.

Neutral Acceptance, the view that death is a reality that is neither feared nor welcomed. (See Note 4).

Other instruments measure death fear and or anxiety but not, always, acceptance and neutrality. For example, the

Death Anxiety Scale measures just that, anxiety about death. Its Likert scale is also more limited to just three responses: "not at all," "somewhat" and "very much." The Collett-Lester Fear of Death Scale "was devised to provide a measure of death anxiety that distinguished between the fear of death and the fear of dying and between fears for oneself and fears for others" (See Note 5).

In comparison with these other instruments, then, one can see that the DAP-R is broader in its conception and assessment. But is it valid in its construction and its application?

To empirically test this, the researchers who created the DAP-R asked ten young, ten middle-aged and ten elderly persons to place each item (i.e. statement on the DAP-R) in each of the five categories where they think it conceptually fit. There was a large amount of agreement on the categories in which the statements were placed: "All 36 items reached our criterion of 70% agreement in classification. In fact, most of the items exceeded the 90% agreement level" (See Note 6).

So, the DAP-R has a significant content validity. This is also seen in the alpha coefficient of internal consistency, a statistical way of measuring whether each statement is consistently related to each other statement and if the responses to the statements are consistent. For example, suppose a person was to strongly agree with the statement, "I hate ice cream." If, on the same instrument, the same respondent were to strongly agree with the statement, "I like chocolate ice cream," the alpha coefficient between the two statements would indicate low internal consistency.

This is not the case with the DAP-R. The alpha coefficients of each of the five dimensions are relatively high and considered reliable. To verify this, the DAP-R was given again to the same 100 young adults, 100 middle aged adults and 100 older adults whose test scores were used to initially determine the content validity and internal consistency of the instrument. The same group, after taking the test again a month after the initial testing, had results that indicated high stability coefficients. This means that, over time, the DAP-R tends to be a helpful way of understanding the lasting views of the respondents.

There tend to be age and gender differences in the attitudes that people bring to their own ideation about death and the reality of their own. "Older adults were significantly more likely to accept death as an escape from life than were both the middle-aged and younger adults. Older adults were also more accepting of life after death, particularly in comparison with middle aged adults" (See Note 7).

It is interesting, and helpful, to note that older adults and younger adults were more likely than the middle aged to strongly agree with the Approach Acceptance dimension. "One plausible interpretation is that young adults may still have residues of beliefs in heaven from childhood. Such beliefs are eroded in middle age but revived in old age" (See Note 8).

Women "were significantly more accepting of life after death and of death as an escape from life than were men. Men, on the other hand, were significantly more prone to avoid all thoughts of death than were women" (See Note 9).

The ways in which these five dimensions can interact are only limited by the variety of human beings that die. A person who has a low fear of death and a high neutral acceptance lives in a much different landscape than one who has a low fear of death and a high escape acceptance. The latter may look forward with relish to the joy of being relieved of burdens while the former may just calmly accept the changes the coming of death brings as one observes the changing of the seasons of the year and watches the flora and fauna become transformed. "Therefore, it is the patterns of different death attitudes rather than the magnitude of a single death attitude that best captures individual differences" (See Note 10).

Neutral Acceptance and Approach Acceptance are, empirically, validated as the most adaptive dimensions in continuing a sense of well being, avoiding depression and living the life that one has left as completely and fully as possible. Approach Acceptance is most akin to what has traditionally been embraced as the "good death" in the *Ars moriendi*, the fourteenth Latin texts that have traditionally informed western cultural constructs of a "good death," and in the Victorian Age (See Note 11). The words, symbols, metaphors and images patients/families use to describe this landscape will be easily related by most caregivers to hymns, readings and prayer/meditation themes.

The Escape Acceptance dimension is also amenable to the consoling and comforting resources available in religious traditions and spirituality. The landscape of Escape Acceptance is very familiar to most care givers. The flora and fauna and the typography will not seem alien to those who are accustomed to working with the dying and, to be effective and thrive in their work, have come to terms with their own mortality.

The most difficult landscape to walk through with our patients/families is Death Avoidance. How can one accompany someone who is denying they are on a journey? Comforting someone who is leaving when they do not acknowledge they are going, requires great sensitivity. Practicing the ministry of presence, being fully alive with the person in the landscape they choose to inhabit, may mean chatting about sports, celebrating family milestones, sharing a television show or just showing up with what Buddhists call "the beginner's mind" to discover, anew, the patients'/families' psychospiritual "field." (I use" field" here in the Gestalt sense).

The implications of traversing each landscape and how the landscapes interact will be explored in the last chapter, "Variegated Landscapes: All Over the Place."

It is not necessary to formally use the DAP-R as an assessment tool. It may seem arbitrary and may invoke hostility if not introduced with humble sensitivity to a situation in which there are so many forms to fill out and professionals making assessments. But keeping these dimensions in mind, if just informally, as caregivers discover the landscapes we share with our patients/families, will help us be more precise and helpful in our interactions. This is why effort was made to establish the content validity and internal consistency of these dimensions. The DAP-R does actually measure, and helps us plumb the depths, of each of its five dimensions.

These five dimensions can be conceptualized as representative of constellations of meaning. If we hear a patient/family say they have an intense fear of death, that alerts us to the fact that they probably also share the other six components or landmarks of that dimension.

In the next five chapters there is an explanation of each of the five dimensions and what religious and spiritual resources are applicable and helpful. I am sure the reader will bring the knowledge of his or her own hymns, readings and prayer/meditation themes to each of the dimensions. The resources are infinite and no one compilation can exhaust their number.

Death Attitude Profile-Revised (DAP-R)
Wong, P.T.P., Reker, G.T., & Gesser, G.

This questionnaire contains a number of statements related to different attitudes toward death. Read each statement carefully, and then decide the extent to which you agree or disagree. For example, an item might read: "Death is a friend." Indicate how well you agree or disagree by circling one of the following: **SA** = strongly agree; **A**= agree; **MA**= moderately agree; **U**= undecided; **MD**= moderately disagree; **D**=disagree; **SD**= strongly disagree. Note that the scales run both from *strongly agree* to *strongly disagree* and from *strongly disagree* to *strongly agree*.

If you strongly agreed with the statement, you would circle **SA**. If you strongly disagreed you would circle **SD**. If you are undecided, circle **U**. However, try to use the undecided category sparingly.

It is important that you work through the statements and answer each one. Many of the statements will seem alike, but all are necessary to show slight differences in attitudes.

1. Death is no doubt a grim experience.

SD D MD U MA A SA

2. The prospects of my own death arouses anxiety in me.

SA A MA U MD D SD

3. I avoid death thoughts at all costs.

SA A MA U MD D SD

4. I believe that I will be in heaven after I die.

SD D MD U MA A SA

5. Death will bring an end to all my troubles.

SD D MD U MA A SA

6. Death should be viewed as a natural, undeniable, avoidable event.

SA A MA U MD D SD.

7. I am disturbed by the finality of death.

SA A MA U MD D SD

8. Death is an entrance to a place of ultimate satisfaction.

SD D MD U MA A SA

9. Death provides an escape from this terrible world.

SA A MA U MD D SD

10. Whenever the thought of death enters my mind, I try to push it away.

SD D MD U MA A SA

11. Death is deliverance from pain and suffering.

SD D MD U MA A SA

12. I always try not to think about death.

SA A MA U MD D SD

13. I believe that heaven will be a much better place than this world.

SA A MA U MD D SD

14. Death is a natural aspect of life.

SA A MA U MD D SD

15. Death is a union with God and eternal bliss.

SD D MD U MA A SA

16. Death brings a promise of a new and glorious life.

SA A MA U MD D SD

17. I would neither fear death nor welcome it.

SA A MA U MD D SD

18. I have an intense fear of death.

SD D MD U MA A SA

19. I avoid thinking about death altogether.

SD D MD U MA A SA

20. The subject of life after death troubles me greatly.

SA A MA U MD D SD

21. The fact that death will mean the end of everything as I know it frightens me.

SA A MA U MD D SD

22. I look forward to a reunion with my loved ones after I die.

SD D MD U MA A SA

23. I view death as a relief from earthly suffering.

SA A MA U MD D SD

24. Death is simply a part of the process of life.

SA A MA U MD D SD

25. I see death as a passage to an eternal and blessed place.

SA A MA U MD D SD

26. I try to have nothing to do with the subject of death.

SD D MD U MA A SA

27. Death offers a wonderful release of the soul.

SD D MD U MA A SA

28. One thing that gives me comfort in facing death is my belief in the afterlife.

SD D MD U MA A SA

29. I see death as a relief from the burden of this life.

SD D MD U MA A SA

30. Death is neither good nor bad.

SA MA U MD D SD

31. I look forward to life after death.

SA A MA U MD D SD

32. The uncertainty of not knowing what happens after death worries me.

SD D MD U MA A SA

Scoring Key for the Death Attitude Profile-Revised

Dimension
Fear of Death (7 items)
1,2,7,18,20,21,32
Death Avoidance (5 items)
3,10,12,19,26
Neutral Acceptance (5 items)
6,14,17,24,30
Approach Acceptance (10 items)
4,8,13,15,16,22,25,27,28,31
Escape Acceptance (5 items)
5,9,11,23,29

Scores for all items are from 1 to 7 in the direction of *strongly disagree (1)* to *strongly agree (7)*. For each dimension, a mean scale score can be computed by dividing the total scale score by the number of items forming each scale.

For further information on the theoretical rationale and the psychometric properties of the scale consult the following source:

Wong, P.T.P., Reker, G.T., & Gesser, G. (1994). Death Attitude Profile-Revised:
"A multidimensional measure of attitudes toward death". in R.A. Neimeyer (Ed.), *Death Anxiety Handbook: Research, Instrumentation, and Application.* (pp. 121-148). Washington, DC: Taylor & Francis.

® Copyright Clearing House. Used by Permission

Chapter 3:

The Landscape of Fear

Fear of death is one of the dimensions measured by the DAP-R. This is a landscape of arctic cold with shivering fear.

This landscape consists of seven statements which represent the parameters of this dimension in the schema being used here:

1. Death is no doubt a grim experience.

2. The prospects of my own death arouse anxiety in me.

7. I am disturbed by the finality of death.

18. I have an intense fear of death.

20. The subject of life after death troubles me greatly.

21. The fact that death will mean the end of everything as I know it frightens me.

32. The uncertainty of not knowing what happens after death worries me.

The number of each statement that corresponds to its number on the DAP-R is placed before each statement.

It is helpful to remember that the presence of a relatively high score of agreement with one statement indicates that the other statements also probably exist in the specific landscape that our patients/families' are traveling through.

Given the traditional notions that are part of the western understanding of what it means to live, and die, i.e. the good death, the family death bed scene, etc., this dimension has many spiritual and religious resources that are available to use.

Five hymnals as well as extensive internet research was done to find hymns that fit the parameters, landmarks and statements of this dimension. The hymns were grouped into these categories Uncertainty, Fear, The End of Everything is Frightening, Anxiety and Death, No Doubt,is a Grim Experience.

SCRIPTURES
   Psalm 13
   Psalm 22: 1-5, 8-11, 14-19
   Psalm 23
   Psalm 27: 1, 4-5, 7-10, 13-14
   Psalm 40: 1-3, 17
   Psalm 42
   Psalm 46: 1-7
   Psalm 55: 1-8
   Psalm 91
   Psalm 121
   Psalm 130
   Psalm 139: 1-18
   Psalm 143: 1-8
   John 14
   Romans 8: 31-39

Hymns

Uncertainty

'Tis So Sweet to Trust in Jesus
A Mighty Fortress Is Our God
All Things Work Out for Good
Ask Ye What Great Thing I Know
Blessed Assurance, Jesus Is Mine
Breathe on Me Breath of God
Christ the Lord Is Risen Today
For Your Glory Reigns
How Firm a Foundation
I Am Thine, O Lord
I Know That My Redeemer Lives
I Know Who Holds Tomorrow
I Love To Tell the Story
I, the Lord
Jerusalem, My Happy Home
Lord of All Hopefulness
Love Divine, All Loves Excelling
My Jesus, I Love Thee
My Redeemer
Ready the Way
Standing on the Promises
Sweet By and By
We Believe in One True God

Fear

Amazing Grace
Be Not Afraid
Come to me, O Weary Traveler
Cristo, Saname (Jesus, Heal Me)
Guide Me, O Thou Great Jehovah
Holy Patron, Thee Saluting
Jesus Is All the World to Me
Jesus Priceless Treasure
Jesus, I Come
Jesus, Lover of My Soul
Jesus, Savior, Pilot Me
Leaning on the Everlasting Arms
No More Death
Saranam, Saranam
Shepherd Me, My God
Take Time to Be Holy
The Kind of Love My Shepherd Is
The Lord's My Shepherd, I'll Not Want
This Alone
Trust and Obey
You Are Mine
You Are Near

The End of Everything is Frightening

All the Way My Savior Leads Me
And Can It Be That I Should Gain
Be Still, My Soul
Creator of the Stars of Night
I Want Jesus to Walk with Me
In Times Like These
It Is Well With My Soul
Jesus Led Me All the Way
Lead Us to the Water
May Nothing Evil Cross This Door
More Love to Thee, O Christ
My Hope is Built
Over the Sunset Mountains
Psalm22: My God, My God (OCP)
Shelter Me, O God
Softly and Tenderly
Tell It to Jesus
The Hand of God Shall Hold You
Thou Hidden Source of Calm Repose
Where He Leads Me
You Are Mine
You Are the Healing

Anxiety
Abide With Me
All Your Anxiety
Be Not Dismayed
Blest Be the Tie That Binds
Come Down, O Love Divine
Dear Creator of Human Kind (adaption of Whittier's
    "Dear Lord and Father of Mankind")
El Shaddai
Guide Me, O Thou Great Jehovah
His Eye is on the Sparrow
In the Garden
It Is Well With My Soul
Pues Si Vivimos ((When We Are Living)
Sun of My Soul Thou Savior Dear
'Tis the Old Ship of Zion
The Lord is my Light
There Is a Longing
When Our Confidence Is Shaken

Death is, no Doubt, a Grim Experience

Children of the Heavenly Father
Come Ye Faithful, Raise the Strain
Follow On
God Be With You 'Til We Meet Again
He Leadeth Me
He Rose
If Thou But Suffer God to Guide Thee
Moment by Moment
My Faith Looks Up to Thee
Near the Cross
O God Our Help in Ages Past
O Love That Wilt Not Let Me Go
O Thou in Whose Presence
Only Trust Him
Out of the Depths I Cry to Thee
Rock of Ages
Room at the Cross for You
Take the Name of Jesus with You
Tell It to Jesus
The Hand of God Shall Hold You
The Old Rugged Cross
There is a Fountain Filled with Blood
Where He Leads Me

Prayer for Uncertainty Aspect

God, our Creator,
    All of our days
Have you loved us,
    Gifted us,
Guided us,
    Graced us
With all good things.

Remind us of your care;
    Wrap us in your love,
Recall for us,
    The goodness of what has been
So we might
    Remember the hope
In the thought of what will be.

Now we find ourselves
    Uncertain of
The future you have
    Opened for us
In the world that is coming.

Establish our feet
    On solid ground;
Anchor us in the faith
    We have proclaimed
And the promises you
    Have given.
As we find our footing,
    As we feel the anchor
Holding fast,
    May the veil
That separates us from your presence
    Be lifted

And our spirits calmed.

We call out to you again,
> Mystery beyond words
To enfold our feelings
> Worries and cares
Into your inner life
> Until our hearts beat
As they did at our beginning,
> As one. **Amen**.

Prayer for Fear Aspect

O God,
    Who calms the raging seas
And soothes the tempests
    Of human hearts,
We are afraid.

The waves we are dreading
    Are washing over us
And threaten
    To overwhelm us
With a drowning
    That makes us flail
Without end
    For a safe harbor.

Soothe our thrashing spirits,
    Ground our feet
On the Rock
    That is higher than I.
Reinforce in us
    The firm conviction
That we are
    More than our bodies
And all that is essential
    About and for us
Is safely kept
    forever in your care.

Calm our souls,
    Still the waters,
Unfold our cramped spirits
    Into your everlasting arms
That our hearts might slow,
    Our breathing relax

As we melt into your
> Steadying presence.
Enfold us,
> O presence beyond words,
In the steady embrace
> Of your love
In the small moments
> Of our journey here
So we might
> Go all the way
Into the future
> With the confidence
You will never
> Let us go. **Amen.**

Prayer for End of Everything is Frightening Aspect

You who are in all
    And has created all,
Who is as close
    As our own breath,
Who knows our fears
    And hears our cries:

Our future seems
    To crush us
With its terrors;
    No longer do
We see it
    As a long
March of days;
    Now it has
Become a burden
    And not a joy.

Where is peace
    In this moment?
Are there
    Any moments of joy
Ahead for us?

Help us find comfort
    In the reality
That the past—
    Is over
The future—
    Is not yet—
This moment is
    The time to live,
        to breathe,
            to laugh,

                    again.
Slow us down,
    Remind us to
Breathe in,
    Breathe out,
Finding in each breath
    the gift of life,
        another moment,
            another chance,
To love, forgive, anticipate ~
    The possibility of
A future greater
    Than our fears,
As close as our breath
    Created by
The One who made us
    And can bring us
Safely home. **Amen.**

Prayer for Anxiety Aspect

O God of the deep night,
    Who knows
Our very soul
    Is anxious,
Dreading what will be,
    Uncertain of your presence
Feeling as if we have been
    Cast aside
From your protection:

Wrap us in the
    Mantle of your love;
O Good Shepherd,
    Whisper words of peace
That linger in our hearts;
    Lift us up where we belong
Out of the depths of our despair
    And set us, again,
In your sight,
    A little lower than the angels.

Slow down our
    Rushing thoughts,
Deepen our breathing
    As we find
Consolation in leaning
    Upon you;
Preserve us from panic
    And help us
Hide ourselves
    Under the sheltering wings
That have given
    Your people

Cover from all anxiety
>	Throughout all generations.

Keep us from
>	Racing into the future
To borrow imagined difficulties
>	From tomorrow
By making your Presence
>	Known in this moment
Through all who care for us
>	With love,
With medicine and skill,
>	With comfort and compassion
So we might know
>	Your answers to our anxieties
Have been continually
>	Before us and beside us.
Within us and around us—constantly.
Amen.

Prayer for Death is a Grim Experience Aspect

We call out to the Deep,
    The depths of mystery
From which we have come,
    And wonder if
There is still yet more
    Of the mystery
To be unfolded for us
    In the future.

We fear being swallowed
    By the deep
And drowning in a
    Desperate struggle
To save ourselves
    From nothingness
And grim obliteration.

We cry out to the deep
    And wait to hear
The welcoming cry
    That this is
Not the end
    But a new beginning.

Our struggle to save
    Ourselves from drowning,
Is keeping us from
    Relaxing into the mystery
Of the deep
    And letting it enfold
Us in the cradling
    Arms of a love
That will not let us go.

Remove the grimness
    Of our vision
And establish in our hearts
    The possibility
Of the goodness
    Still yet to come.

Remind us that
    Gazing into
The depths of our own soul
    Is but a way
Of looking into eternity
    To see beauty
And calmness,
    Serenity and peace
Reflected back from the One
    Who commands the deep
And has a limitless reservoir
    Of life for all
Who enter into rest. **Amen**.

Chapter Four

The Landscape of Death Avoidance

This landscape is the sunniest of all. Everything is wonderful here. The flowers are perfect, the lawns are immaculate, the mountains are perfectly sculpted and dotted with patches of snow in artful patterns.

Things are too perfect, in fact. All the flowers are fake, the lawns are artificial and the mountains are from the make believe land of the movie set.

Fear is not the problem here but anxiety. Fear is something that can be felt, in this way of understanding the human psyche, while anxiety is more deeply rooted and is masked. There is so much anxiety about death that the patient has constructed a hardened defensive barrier of denial.

The result is that the patient may have lost all of her hair and may have a central line implanted in order to receive medicine, but the nearness of death is denied. This can be especially frustrating to caregivers who want each patient to have time to reconcile themselves with their terminal diagnosis, tie up any loose ends of their life and leave with as much hope and as little pain and suffering as possible.

It is commonly heard among end of life caregivers that such and such patient is in denial. It is said with a kind of sad tone as if it would be better for them to wake up and prepare themselves and their loved ones for the exit. It is also wearing on the caregivers to have to be indirect about the issue of the impending death and walk on eggshells.

The unalterable reality is that this is the patient's journey. They have chosen this orientation toward death for good reasons and we have to build on the good reasons they have for "being in denial." Seeing the indirection about death as being for the benefit of the patient might help reframe it in a more helpful and healthy context for caregivers.

Another way of saying this is that there is spirituality in denial that we have not plumbed very deeply. This spirituality is based on protection and safe harbor. The knowledge of their own death is too much for them to handle and their denial mechanisms are a means of providing themselves shelter and comfort. It may be an artificial world but it is the landscape that the patient has chosen and our task is, as they say with Alzheimer's patients, to "join the journey."

The five statements which comprise Death Avoidance on the DAP-R are:

19. I avoid thinking about death altogether.

12. I always try not to think about death.

26. I try to have nothing to do with the subject of death.

3. I avoid death thoughts at all cost.

10. Whenever the thought of death enters my mind, I try to push it away.

Accompanying those in this landscape is not difficult in any technical sense. Whatever meaning system they are using to distract themselves and keep the awful knowledge of their own mortality at bay, becomes the basis for our interactions.

If they are sports fans, our responses are geared toward sports. If they are passionate about their grandchildren, our responses are based on their pride and good feelings about their family. If they enjoy following politics, we can listen as they fulminate about the latest news from that world.

That doesn't mean we can't ask questions geared toward a life review but the questions must come from the details of the landscapes they exist in. For example, if they show a caregiver a picture of a grandchild, that can become an opportunity to ask if they remember when their own children were that young and what that time of their life was like.

Open ended questions are always helpful in trying to orient the death avoidant patient no matter how artificial their landscape. For example, a caregiver could ask about how they feel about being in a nursing home or how it feels to them to receive get well cards. Denial cannot be addressed directly because the patient needs the protection and a straightforward approach would just increase the strength of the denial mechanisms.

I find it to generally be true that those who are death avoidant either have no formal religious participation or a very conventional religious practice. By conventional I mean they have not integrated their religious belief system into the realities of their daily lives. Religious practice has become a habit but has not had much impact on the construction of their character. One can surmise that many in this landscape will not find much use for traditional religious themes, hymns, prayers, readings or meditations.

If they are part of a liturgical tradition which ritualizes and recognizes the seasons of the church year, it might be helpful to celebrate the office of the day or read the reading of the day or sing a song for/with them from that particular season. Those whose religious belief is more free form can be accompanied by prayers, readings and hymns/songs which emphasize protection, safety, comfort and the sheltering presence of God.

SCRIPTURES
Psalm 61: 1-5
Psalm 62: 1-2, 5-8
Psalm 63: 1-8
Psalm 91

Psalm 18: 1-3
Psalm 36: 5-10
Psalm 61: 1-4

Hymns

PROTECTION

'Tis So Sweet to Trust in Jesus
A Mighty Fortress is Our God
All Things Work Out For Good
Angel Hymn for Protection
Blessed Assurance
Deep Down in My Soul
Farther Along
God Will Take Care of You
He Leadeth Me
How Firm a Foundation
I am His and He is Mine
I Have Loved You
I Know Who Holds Tomorrow
I Was in His Mind
I'll Fly Away
Immortal, Invisible, God Only Wise
It Is Well With My Soul
Jesus Led Me All the Way
My God and I
My Hope Is Built
Saranam, Saranam
Something Good is Going to Happy to You
Standing on the Promises
Surely Goodness and Mercy
This Little Light of Mine
Trust and Obey
You Are All We Have

SHELTERING

A Mighty Fortress is Our God
A Safe Stronghold Our God is Still
All Praise to Him Who Dwells in Bliss
As the Bird Flies Home
Beneath His Sheltering Wings
Dear Father, to Thy Mercy Seat
Defend Me, Lord, From Shame
Dread Jehovah, God of Nations
Flee as a Bird
Fly to Thy Refuge
God is a Stronghold and a Tower
God is our Refuge
God is our Refuge and Our Strength
God Will our Strength and Refuge Prove
Hail, Sovereign Love
He Shields from the Storms of Life
He That Hath Made His Refuge God
He Will Hide Me
Hear, Lord, the Voice of My Complaint
Hear, O Lord, Our Supplication
Hide Me (Bowyer)
Hide Me (Crosby)
Hide Thou Me
Hiding in Thee
How Blest the Man Who Thoughtfully
In the Midst of Earthly Life
In the Secret of His Presence
In the Secret Place of God
In the Shadow of His Wings
In Thy Holy Keeping
Jehovah is My Light
Just Are Thy Ways
Leaning Upon My Father's Arm

Let My Life Be Hid in Thee
Like a Bird to Thee
Long Did I Toil
Lord, Hear Me in Distress
Lord, Hear the Right
Lord, in Thee am I Confiding
Make Haste, O My God, to Deliver
May Thy Church Our Shelter Be
My god! Permit My Tongue
My God, in Whom Are All the Springs
My Heart's Dear Home
My High Tower
My Refuge
My Refuge Is the God of Love
My Soul is Grieved
My Soul with Expectation
My Spirit Looks to God Alone
My Trust Is in the Lord
Now from the Roaring Lion's Rage
O Fly to Him
O God Be Merciful to Me
O God, Be Merciful
O God, Give Ear
O God, My Refuge, Hear My Cries
O God, Regard My Humble Plea
O Happy Nation
O Lord Most High
O Lord, Give Ear unto My Voice
O Lord, Our Father, Shall We Be Confounded?
O Lord, Thou Judge
O Save Me By Thy Name
Oh, What Wilt Thou Do?
On Eagles' Wings
Our God, to Whom We Turn
Protect and Save Me, O My God
Safe in Jehovah's Keeping

Save Me, O Lord, from Every Foe
Sweetly Resting
The Good Man's Steps Are Led Aright
The Man Who Once has Found Abode
There Is a Safe and Secret Place
Thou Art My Hiding Place, O Lord
Though Troubles Great O'ereshadow Me
To God My Earnest Voice I Raise
To the Hills I Life Mine Eyes
To Thee, O Lord, I Humbly Cry
We Love, Thee Lord, and We Adore
When In the Hour of Utmost Need
When Morning Lights the Eastern Skies
Ye Humble Souls, Approach Your God

SAFE HARBOR

Brighten the Corner
Jesus, Savior, Pilot Me
Safe Harbor by Bryan Duncan
Safe Within the Vail
Sailing Into Port
This Old Ship of Zion

PRAYERS

We call out in gratitude,
    To the One who has made us,
        kept us
            guided us:
You alone have
    Provided protection,
        shelter,
            safe harbor
Our entire lives.

Continue to enfold us,
    In your loving arms
So we might
    Find something good
In every day and moment.

Keep us from
    The terrors of the night
So we might enjoy
    The benefits of your light
Until we rejoice
    Forever in your Presence.
Amen.

We thank you,
    O God,
For the gifts
    Of our families,
        friends
            and loved ones.

Keep reminding us
    Of the goodness of life,
The wonder of love
    And the splendor
Of this moment.

Save us from all
    Negativity and resignation
To weakness of spirit
    And help us
Cling to your light.

Fix our focus
    On all that is good,
        perfect
            and healing
So we might
    Grow in spirit,
Remain under your wings
    And claim our heritage
As being made
    Just a little lower
Than the angels. **Amen**.

Protect us, O Lord,
    From all that
Would threaten us
    With uneasiness
And fearfulness.

Wrap us in your wings
    That we might
Find shelter and repose
    From all fright
And discomfort.

Usher us into
    Your everlasting presence
Until our serenity
    Here is grounded
Completely in your peace.

Thanks for all that has been,
    all that is
        and all that will be.
Grant us the faith
    To declare it all
Good and perfect
    So we might
Abide in your love
    And live, today,
In your light. **Amen**.

We give thanks
    O God of the depths,
That you give us
    Safety and shelter
From all the storms
    That have afflicted others.

Make us ever more aware
    Of your goodness to us,
So our thankfulness
    Will create a habit
That leads to abundant
    Living for us.

Remove all traces
    Of darkness
From our souls
    And lead us
Ever closer to your light.

Anchor us staunchly
    In the safe harbor
Of your divine protection;
    Establish in us
Your ever victorious light
    That we might
Be more than conquerors
    In all things. **Amen**.

O God, who is light
    And in whom
There is no darkness
    at all:
Wrap our minds
    Around the wonder
Of your loving kindness
    To us and all creatures.

Focus our vision
    On the wonders
Of what can be
    Our life here
As a foretaste
    Of what is to come.

Sharpen our awareness
    Of all your mercies
To us until
    We are completely
Aware of every breath
    As a gift from you.

With gratitude
    For all you have done,
Awareness of the
    Wonder of this moment
And hope for
    Ever increasing love,
We await more
    Now and always. **Amen.**

Chapter Five

The Landscape of Neutral Acceptance

Every summer we travel to Glen Arbor, Michigan and rent a house big enough to vacation with the entire family. Traveling north on Interstate 75, right near Gaylord, Michigan, the ecology of the landscape changes from deciduous forest to pine forest. If one is not paying attention, it seems to happen abruptly. But a closer examination reveals that the change is gradual; one landscape merges seamlessly into the other.

Small pine trees are scattered in the deciduous ecology. The closer one travels to the pine forest zone, the bigger the pine trees become. One can almost envision the increasingly larger pine trees as representing the stairs that lead up to the new landscape.

This is the way the patients and their families and/or loved one in this landscape understand death. It is part of the same landscape. Death and life are all part of existence. They go together like Yin and Yang.

In fact, this landscape is most amenable to Eastern religious belief systems and spirituality practices. The duality of Western thinking, explicated in Chapter One, "Preparing to Join the Journey," is foreign to this understanding. The wisdom tradition in the Old Testament, particularly Ecclesiastes 3: 1-9, is most applicable. There is a time for every purpose: a time to die, and a time to live.

Also, in the traditions of the First Peoples there is the view that all of existence is a circle and we end at our beginning (See Note One). The point of death on the circle upon which we come "full circle" is also the point of life.

The landscape of neutral acceptance is created by these landmarks or statements:

6. Death should be viewed as a natural, undeniable, and unavoidable event.

14. Death is natural aspect of life.

17. I would neither fear death nor welcome it.

24. Death is simply a part of the process of life.

30. Death is neither good nor bad.

I have worked with many people who are traveling through this landscape. They calmly accept that the landscape is changing. They sometimes feel a little helpless about the process but they seem to understand, at some level, it is part of what it means to be human, to be creatures and be finite.

This opens up some possibilities that are not often commonly explored in the West. To be able to contemplate one's own death makes it possible to die consciously. This is represented by the Tibetan concept of "The Transference of Consciousness on Death' and the phowa ceremony.

It would be simplistic and reductionist to say they are exactly similar, but in Christian theology there is the concept that Jesus of Nazareth did not have his life taken from him, but he gave it up. Jewish people are encouraged to die witht the words of the Shema on their lips. Some depictions of the death of the Buddha also indicate he willfully gave his life up [(See Note Two)](See Note Two).

There comes a time in one's journey when death is no longer the enemy but a friend. One's body is worn out, one's spirit is exhausted and there is a longing for a deep rest. Perhaps this is the reason why death is called an angel or some sort of supernatural being in many of the world's most popular religions.

Conscious dying may seem a little strange on first glance but it is not so odd when we remember the number of times in which a dying patient will deliberately concentrate on staying alive until a wedding or a special birthday or other marker event. They may not be fully conscious but they are aware, on some level, of how they want to die and they exert their will. It is also not uncommon for those at the end of life, who want to die alone, to wait until they are alone to die. Conversely, I have experienced the dying waiting until all the family members have arrived to release their life.

Because this is not a predominant theme in Western ways of envisioning death, there are not as many resources available as far as hymnody or scriptures. So, I have listed the hymns and scripture that I have found that apply to this, but also included other readings that might be helpful and meaningful.

SCRIPTURES

Ecclesiastes 3: 1-9
Song of Solomon 2: 11-13c
Mark 4: 26-29
Psalm 104: 1-33

HYMNS

A Long, Long Way the Sea-Winds Blow
A Promise Through the Ages Rings
All Beautiful the March of Days
Bring, O Morn, Thy Music
Come Sunday
Dark of Winter
Dear Weaver of Our Lives' Design
Every Night and Every Morn
Have I Not Known
Hymn of Promise
I Am That Great and Fiery Force
I Know This Rose Will Open
I Sought the Wood in Summer
Immortal Love
In Sweet Fields of Autumn
It is Something to Have Wept
Lady of the Seasons' Laughter
Let Hope and Sorrow Now United
Let It Be a Dance
No Longer Forward nor Behind
Now I Recall My Childhood
Now on Land and Sea Descending
O Life That Maketh all Things New
Parable
Sakura
Sing of Living, Sing of Dying
Singer of Life
Songs of Spirit
The Ceaseless Flow of Endless Time
The Leaf Unfurling
The Sun at High Noon
The Wind of Change Forever Blown

The World Stand Out on either Side
This Is the Truth That Passes Understanding
To See the World
View the Starry Realm
We Celebrate the Web of Life
We Laugh, We Cry
When Darkness Nears
When Our Confidence is Shaken
When Shall We Learn
Where My Free Spirit Onward Leads
Wild Waves of Storm

READINGS

Look to this day!
For it is life, the very life of life.
In its brief course lie all the
    verities
And realities of existence:
    The bliss of growth,
    The glory of action,
    The splendor of beauty;
For yesterday is but a dream,
And tomorrow is only a vision;
But today, well lived, makes every
    Yesterday
A dream of happiness
And every tomorrow a vision of
    hope.
Look well, therefore, to this day.

Attributed to Kalidasa

And I have felt a presence that
    disturbs me with the joy of
    elevated thoughts;
A sense sublime of something far
    more deeply interfused,
Whose dwelling is the light of
    setting suns,
And the round ocean and the
    living air,
A motion and a spirit, that impels
All thinking things, all objects of
    all thought,
And rolls through all things.

William Wordsworth

May the glory of the passing away
    of autumn
    lie about us
    fresh gold
    for a time.
And when the dark comes, and
    the cold
May we remember how today we
    stand in glory,
How we walk in bounty
    heaped upon earth's dark carpet,
How we move knee deep in
    abundance
Flung against night's winter
    curtain.
We are thankful for its coming
    and for its passing.

Let it be.

Barbara J. Pescan used by permission

Immortality

It is eternity now.
I am in the midst of it.

It is about me, in the sunshine,
I am in it, as the butterfly in the
    night-laden air.

Nothing has to come,
It is now.

Now is eternity,
Now is the immortal life.

Richard Jeffries

The Stream of Life

The same stream of life that runs through my veins night and day runs through the world and dances in rhythmic measures.

It is the same life that shoots in joy through the dust of the earth in numberless blades of grass and breaks into tumultuous waves of lawns and flowers.

It is the same life that is rocked in the ocean-cradle of birth and death, in ebb and in flow.

Rabindranath Tagore

Harbingers of Frost

Autumn, we know,
Is life en route to death.
The asters are but harbingers of
    frost.

The trees, flaunting their colors at
    the sky,
In other times will follow where
    the leaves have fallen,
And so shall we.

Yet other lives will come.
So may we know, accept, embrace,
The mystery of life we hold a
    while.

Nor mourn that it outgrows each
    separate self, but still rejoice
    that we may have our day.

Lift high our colors to the sky!
    and give,
In our time, fresh glory to the
    earth.

Robert T. Weston Used by Permission

October's Raspberries

Red surprise
    D
    R
    I
    Z
    Z
    L
    E
    D
With October's
    Graces.

Intense flavors
    Bursting
With summer's
    Traces.

Birds complaining
    Chirping
Of stolen
    Cases.

Hiding treasures
    Shirking
In darkened
    Places.

Nature's bounty
    Fading
In measured
    Paces

Winter's coming
    Waxing

In Fall's
   Waning.
Keith A. Rasey

To Free the Heart

Through dreary sodden days
The fields sponged up
The graying skies.

And now the sun
Lies soft as birth again
As if the earth had just begun.

And blossoms on the vines
Designed in spring
Come out to sing again.

And everywhere the ripening
Pushes falling leaves apart
To free the heart
For freshening.

As through the seasons
Of our years

Becoming
Often waits the nourishment
Of tears.

Francis C. Anderson Jr.

Beyond Words

Existence is beyond the power of
words to define:
Terms may be used but are none
of them absolute.
In the beginning of heaven and
earth there were no words,
Words come out of the womb of
Matter;
And whether we dispassionately see
to the core of life or passionately see
the surface, the core and the surface
are essentially the same,
Words making them see different only to express appearance.
If name be needed, wonder names
them both; from wonder to wonder existence opens.

Lao-Tse

Life Again

Out of the dusk a shadow,
Then, a spark.

Out of the cloud a silence,
Then, a lark.

Out of the heart, a rapture,
Then, a pain.

Out of the dead, cold ashes,
Life again.

John Banister Tabb

I
What we call a beginning is often
    the end
And to make an end is to make a
    beginning.
The end is where we start from.

II
We shall not cease from
    Exploration
and the end of all our exploring
will be to arrive where we started
and know the place for the first
    time.

T. S. Eliot "Four Quartets" ®Harcourt Brace Jovanovic, Inc. used by permission

The Tao

Before creation a presence existed,
Self-contained, complete,
    formless, voiceless, mateless,
    changeless,
Which pervaded itself with
    Unending motherhood.

Though there can be name
    for it,
I have called it the "way of
    life."

Perhaps I should have called it
    "the fullness of life,"
Since fullness implies widening
    into space,
Implies still further widening,
Implies widening until the circle
    is whole.
In this sense
The way of life is fulfilled,
Heaven is fulfilled,
Earth is fulfilled,
And a fit person also is fulfilled.

These are the four amplitudes of
    the universe
And a fit person is one of them.

People rounding the way of
    earth,
Earth rounding the way of
    heaven,
Heaven rounding the way of life

Till the circle is full.
Lao-Tse

PRAYERS
Eternal, Immutable God,
    Through all the seasons
Of our lives
    You have brought us through.
In spring
    You gave us
The bounty of youth;
In summer
    You gave us
The fullness of life;
In fall
    You gave us
The quickening ripeness.

Now we are in winter.
    Help us see
In this stark season
    That there is still
Beauty and serenity;
    Show us
You are still here
    With us
Preparing us
    For the eternal spring. **Amen.**

Where have the years gone,
    O Timeless God?
Just yesterday
    We were learning
To walk and run
    And here we are
Slowed down
    Waiting for this season
To reach its culmination.

Our years have
>   Hurried by
And now we wait
>   For the fullness
Of your presence.

Help us,
>   look you in the face,
O Merciful God,
>   So we might
Keep our vision
>   On the goal
Of moving from this place
>   To your place.

Remind us of
>   The ways you
Made a path
>   In all the past days
So we might
>   Have confidence
You have planned
>   Celebrations to welcome
Us to our forever home
>   With you. **Amen**.

Our days have been sweet
>   O God of Abundant life;
You have cracked open
>   The goodness of this world
For us to taste
>   The marrow
That has nourished
>   All our days
And made us
>   Grateful for all

That has been.

Now, we seek to move
    To your place
Where the seasons
    Are all wonderful
And the sweetness
    Goes on and on.

Give us faith
    That this move
Will be easy
    And will be
Accomplished in,
    What is for you,
A twinkling of the eye.

Grant us patience
    As we wait
In the winter
    Of our days
For our time
    Here to be complete.

Reconcile us to
    The idea that
Your timing is
    Perfect
And you, yourself,
    Will welcome us
Home. **Amen.**

As the crocus,
    Appears suddenly
Even when the
    Chill is still in the air,

May our transition
    Into the fullness
Of your presence
    Just as miraculously
Suddenly and painlessly
    Be accomplished
O God of all good things.

Bring us out of this
    Season of winter
And into the
    Surprising beauty
Of a renewed spring.

We have seen
    You do this
Over and over
    Again
Throughout the years
    And believe it
Will not be
    Difficult for you
To do for us.

Grant us the faith
    To harbor
Our hopes
    For a smooth
Transition until
    We receive
The sign from you
    O God,
That the time is right
    And you are
Completely ready
    For us to move

On and in. **Amen**.

Finally, has winter
    Come for us
O Lord of
    All creatures
And seasons of life.

We knew it was
    Coming for
We know there
    Is a season
For every purpose
    Under heaven.

Steady our faith
    That you are
Just as much
    In charge of winter
As you are
    Of spring,
O renewing God.

Help us put
    Our trust in you
To bring ease
    Of living
In this time
    Of our lives;
Grant us faith
    That this season
Of change and transition
    Is something you
Have created as
    Part of what
It means to be
    Made a little

Lower than the angels.

Keep us ready
> To move on

Without rushing you
> As you prepare

Our place.
> When you deem

It is our time
> To move on,

Lead us by your love,
> Guide us

With your presence
> And encourage us

With a hope
> That will not

Let us go
> Until we are

Safely in your arms. **Amen**

Internet sites for more resources pertaining to this landscape

http://www.the-great-adventure.com/prayers_readings_practices/prayers_and_readings.html
http://www.nhpco.org/templates/1/homepage.cfm
http://www.hospicenet.org/html/watch.html

Chapter Six

The Landscape of Approach Acceptance

This landscape, along with Neutral Acceptance, is probably the one that end of life caregivers would call, "The Good Death" in the tradition of *Ars Moriendi* or even, more cogently, the Victorian ideal. This is the place where all deserve to die, in acceptance, hope, and composure, surrounded by family, to whom they have had time to say good bye, and free of pain.

In my imagination I envision this landscape as a slow, steady declining hill that leads to the most beautiful valley possible. The river running through the valley is a peaceful blue and the waters are rolling just enough to provide abundant life to all the living creatures that depend upon the river for life.

Diagnoses that would seem to be most likely to be found in this landscape including those in which there has been a long slow gradual decline such as many cancers or failure to thrive. The patients and families traveling through this landscape, in as much as they are looking forward to the life that comes after this one and are imbued with the ideals of western culture, typically believe in life after death in traditional ways.

The many landmark statements that comprise this landscape or domain on the DAP-R are:

4. I believe I will be in heaven after I die.

8. Death is an entrance to a place of ultimate satisfaction.

13. I believe that heaven will be a much better place than this world.

15. Death is a union with God and eternal bliss.

16. Death brings a promise of a new and glorious life.

22. I look forward to a reunion with my loved ones after I die.

25. I see death as a passage to an eternal and blessed place.

27. Death offers a wonderful release of the soul.

28. One thing that gives me comfort in facing death is my belief in the afterlife.

31. I look forward to life after death.

People and families in this landscape are amenable to all the traditional comforts, nostrums and resources of the various Judeo-Christian traditions. They are generally grateful for the comfort of their faith and benefit from having it celebrated and reinforced.

It may be helpful here to again note that those in this landscape report having the greatest sense of well being, are more free from depression and more capable of adapting to live as fully and completely as they can.

Because there are so many statements in this landscape/domain, I have studied the statements and summed them up with these themes: Comfort, Reunion, Wonderful Release, Promise of New Life and Looking Forward to Heaven.

Scriptures
Ps. 36: 7-9
Ps. 46
Ps. 52: 8-9
Ps. 93
Ps. 97
Ps. 98
Ps. 100
Ps. 107: 1-9
Ps. 111

Ps. 113
Ps. 116
Ps. 121
Ps. 126
Ps. 145
John 14
John 15: 1-17
Romans 8: 18-25, 28, 31-31, 35-39
Hebrews 11: 1-16
Hebrews 12: 1-2
I Peter 1: 3-5
II Peter 3 8-13
Revelation 3: 20-21
Revelation 19: 6-9
Revelation 21: 1-7, 9-27
Revelation 22: 1-5

Hymns

COMFORT

'Tis So Sweet To Trust in Jesus
A Mighty Fortress Is Our God
Abide With Me
All Things Work Out for Good
And Can It Be That I Should Gain
Ave Maria
Be Still and Know That I am God
Canticle of Remembrance
Closer Walk With Thee
Come Down, O Love Divine
Come To Me
Comfort, Comfort, O My People
Do Lord, Remember Me
Endless Is Your Love
Eye Has Not Seen
For All the Saints
For You Are My God
God Will Take Care of You
Here I Am
His Name Is Wonderful
How Great Thou Art
I Know That My Redeemer Lives
I Need Thee Every Hour
I Stand Amazed in the Presence
I Will Trust in the Lord
I've Got Peace Like a River
In Every Age
In Times Like These
Jesus, Heal Us
Jesus, Savior, Pilot Me
Jesus Lover Of My Soul

Just As I Am
Kum Ba Yah
Leaning on the Everlasting Arms
Like A Shepherd
Love Divine, All Loves Excelling
Near To Thy Heart
O God Our Help in Ages Past
O Sacred Head Now Wounded
On Eagles' Wings
Only a Shadow
Our Great Savior
Our God Is Rich in Love
Parable (OCP)
Part in Peace
Pass Me Not
Praise, O My Heart, To You
Rock of Ages
Save Your People
Savior, Like a Shepherd Lead Us
Send Us Your Spirit
Shalom
Shelter Me, O God
Shepherd of My Heart
Song of Farewell
Spirit of Life
Standing on the Promises
Sun of My Soul
Take the Name of Jesus With You
Tell It To Jesus
The Lord's My Shepherd
The Strife is O'er the Battle Won
Though The Mountains My Fall
Victory In Jesus
Where He Leads Me
Where My Father Lives
With A Shepherd's Care

You Are Near

REUNION

'Tis the Old Ship of Zion
All Hail the Power of Jesus Name
All I Ask of You
Beautiful Beckoning Hands
Blest Be the Tie That Binds
Blow Ye the Trumpet Blow
Come Let Us Join Our Friends Above
For All the Saints
Go In Peace
God Be With You
Hallelujah, What A Savior
In Paradisum
Jerusalem, My Happy Home
Let Saints on Earth In Concert Sing
Maranatha
Shall We Gather at the River?
Song of Farewell
Sooner or Later
The Church's One Foundation
We'll Never Say Goodbye
We Shall Rise Again
When the Roll Is Called Up Yonder
Will the Circle Be Unbroken

WONDERFUL RELEASE

Be Still, My Soul
Christ Arose
Christ Jesus Lay in Death's Strong Bonds
Crown Him With Many Crowns
Fix Me, Jesus
I am Thine, O Lord
I'll Fly Away
In the Garden
Jesu, Dulci Memoria
Jesus, I Come
Leave It There
Love That Wilt Not Let Me Go
Marching to Zion
On Eagles' Wings
O Sons and Daughters, Let us Sing
Soon and Very Soon
Stand Up For Jesus
Sweet Hour of Prayer
Swing Low, Sweet Chariot
The Old Rugged Cross
The Strife's O'er, the Battle Done
The Head the Once Was Crowned
There is a Fountain
Turn Your Eyes Upon Jesus
Up From The Grave He Arose
Way Over Yonder
Wonderful Words of Life

PROMISE OF NEW LIFE

'Tis So Sweet to Trust in Jesus
Breathe on Me, Breath of God
Christ the Lord Is Risen Today
Cristo Vive
El Shaddai
Fight the Good Fight
Have Thine Own Way, Lord
He Lives
Heaven Came Down and Filled My Soul
How Lovely Is Your Dwelling Place
I Have Loved You
Isaiah 49 (OCP)
Jesus Christ is Risen Today
Just As I Am
Now the Green Blade Riseth
O Day of Light and Gladness
Only Trust Him
Our Hope Is In the Lord
Standing on the Promises
Show Us the Path of Life
The King of Love My Shepherd Is
The Lord Is My Hope
The Lord Is My Shepherd
Where He Leads I'll Follow

DEATH AS PASSAGE TO BETTER PLACE

All the Way My Savior Leads Me
Breathe on Me Breath of God
He Leadeth Me
How Lovely Is Your Dwelling
I'm On My Way
I, the Lord
Joyful is the Dark
Must Jesus Bear the Cross Alone
My Faith Looks Up To Thee
Rock of Ages
Shall We Gather At the River?
Surely Goodness and Mercy
Take Time To Be Holy
The Hand of God Shall Hold You
The Old Rugged Cross
When We All Get to Heaven
Why Do We Mourn Departing Friends?
On Jordan's Stormy Banks

LOOKING FORWARD TO HEAVEN

All the Way My Savior Leads Me
Be Thou My Vision
Beyond the Moon and Stars
Blessed Assurance
Higher Ground
I Love To Tell the Story
I Stand Amazed in the Presence
I'll Fly Away
I've Got a New Name
In My Heart There Rings a Melody
Jesus Led Me All the Way
Lord, You Have Come to the Lakeshore
My Jesus, I Love Thee
Saved By Grace
Steal Away to Jesus
Victory in Jesus
We're Marching to Zion
When We All Get To Heaven

PRAYERS ON COMFORT:

O Great and All loving God,
    The author of Life,
Victor over death,
    We are grateful
For the comfort given to us
    In the promise of heaven
And the hope for life
        Everlasting.

The sure knowledge
    That you are with us
Calms our spirits,
    Steadies our souls
And quickens our hearts.

We give thanks
    For the path
You have paved
    Into the world
That you have
    Created and sustained for us.

We look forward
    To seeing you
Face to face
    And living
In our Eternal Home
    With you
And all the saints
    Through Jesus, the Christ
Who lives and reigns
    With you in the unity
Of the Holy Spirit,
    Now and forever. **Amen.**

Ground of our Being,
    Promise of our deliverance
From brokenness and death,
    Lift us on eagles' wings
That we might
    Fly to the heights
Where you, yourself,
    Personally comfort
And welcome us
Into our inheritance
    Of all heaven's glories.

Wean us from
    The brokenness
Of this world;
    Complete in us
The work you began
    When creation was begun
And bestow upon us
    All the benefits of heaven.

This we pray,
    In the name
Of Jesus Christ our Lord,
    Who has called us his own
And will safely
    Shepherd us all the way
home. **Amen.**

PRAYERS FOR PROMISE OF NEW LIFE

O God who has promised
    Good to all
Who trust in
    Your Grace
And the final triumph
    Of your will
For all creation,
    We give you thanks
For the promise of new life
    You have given us
In the perfector
    Of our faith
Jesus Christ , our Lord.

May the promise of heaven
    Sustain us in this hour
And nurture the patience
    We need
To be more
    Than conquerors
In all situations. **Amen**

Standing on your promises
    O God,
We can see
    The heights you have
Made us for;
    The trials of the present hour
Are but a trifling moment
    Compared to what
You have promised
    To prepare for us.

Wrap the promises
    Of heaven
Around our hearts
    When we grow
Weary of our journey.
    Renew our souls
By giving us a vision
    Of what has
Been promised for us
    And for all
Who love you.

Redeem us from
    Nearsightedness
And pour out
    The treasures of heaven
So we might
    See your promises
Fulfilled in the
    Face of your Son,
Jesus of Nazareth,
    In whose name we pray.
Amen.

DEATH AS PASSAGE TO A BETTER PLACE

Through the narrows
    Of illness and despair,
        Pilot us,
O Captain of our souls,
    To that blessed
Place where we have
    Eternal rest
And see you face to face.
Grant us the sure faith
    That this moment
Is pregnant
    With the possibilities
Of new life.
    Reassure us
That our present
    Burdens and suffering
Are the birth pains
    Of a new world
You are creating
    For us in the heavens
With you and
    All the angels
Who have already
    Crossed over
Through the narrow passageways
    That lead to life eternal. **Amen.**

O God, who goes before us,
    Thanks for showing
Us the way
    Through the desert
Into the promised land.

Our journey has
    Not always been smooth,
It has not always been easy—
    And the passageway
Has sometimes
    Seemed narrow
But we have faith
    It leads to an
Eternal and blessed place.

Confirm us in our faith,
    Grant us safe passage
That we might arrive
    Upon the heights
You have made for us
    And share with the angels
The fulfillment of all days
    So our rest
Is final and our journey
    Complete. **Amen.**

PRAYERS ABOUT REUNION WITH LOVED ONES

Lord of all ages,
    Creator of all worlds,
Our loved ones
    Are beckoning us onward
To join them
    And all the saints
In eternal choruses
    Of thanksgiving.

O Welcoming God,
    We are coming
To take our seat
    At the great banquet
And partake of the manna
    That eternally satisfies.

We hear them call,
    We see them
Urge us homeward,
    And we are coming
Closer and closer
    To our moment
Of departure for the feast.

Thanks for telling them
    We are coming,
O Lord of the Banquet;
    Reunite us
In an eternal embrace
    That never ends
In the world without end. **Amen**

O God who has shared our flesh
    And knows of how
Our flesh cries
    Out to be reunited
With all from whom we come,
    Smooth our way home.

Embrace us in person,
    O Mothering God,
Reconnect us with
    All who have
Paved our way homeward
    With their love
Faith, hope and joy.

Gather us together,
    As one Body
So the joys of reunion
    Swallow the pain
Of Separation
    In the victory
Of homecoming celebration.

This we ask
    In the name
Of the One
    Who presides
At the reunion banquet
    And who dwells
In eternal union
    With the Creator
And Sustainer. **Amen**

PRAYERS ABOUT DEATH AS A WONDERFUL RELEASE:

Our souls long for you,
    O God
As a deer pants
    For water.

You are our beloved
    And the time
Of our betrothal
    Is close at hand.

Draw us to yourself,
    O loving God;
Release our souls,
    From their bodily
Chains with the earth
    And unite us
With you forever.

How wonderful,
    How marvelous
Shall be the rejoicing
    At the hour
Our soul springs
    Into your arms
And we are free
    From suffering.

Thanks for this possibility
    But thanks, even more,
For the reality
    Of a love
That cannot be
    Quenched by

Death, time or dis-ease
    Due to the
Love of the Bridegroom,
    Jesus Christ, our Lord. **Amen**

O You who are beyond the stars,
    The One who spins
Galaxies and births worlds,
    Draw us close to yourself
And release us
    Again, to the womb of eternity.

We long to experience,
    The passageway
That leads us
    To life renewed;
Remind us that
    Our sufferings here
Are the labor pains
    Of a new life
Being born in and through us
    That we might
Be better able
    To face our fear
And our pain.

We know you
    Are the One,
Who wrings hope
    Out of despair
And new life
    Where there is
Only barrenness and sorrow.

Accomplish this for us,
    O Wonderful God,

That we might
> Feel the release
From our pain
> And the joy
At our arrival
> In the place
You are creating
> For us
Through our suffering.

This we ask
> In the name
Of the God
> Who suffered for us
To create possibilities
> Out of dead ends
And eternity
> In each soul,
Jesus Christ, our Lord. **Amen**

Chapter Seven

The Landscape of Escape Acceptance

This landscape can be conceived as a desert with a beautiful oasis within sight. Alternatively, it can be envisioned as a rocky mountain path which leads to the most verdant, fertile, vertiginous meadow imaginable.

It is easy to intuit that patients with certain hospice diagnoses are most likely to predominate in this landscape. Parkinson's and Alzheimer's immediately come to mind. A long, suffering journey results in a pining for a better future in which one can escape suffering and hope for a restored life. Alternatively, a diagnosis which involves acute pain which has been difficult to control with medication, may also fit here.

The statements that comprise this domain/landscape are:

5. Death will bring an end to all my troubles.

9. Death provides an escape from this terrible world.

11. Death is deliverance from pain and suffering.

23. I view death as a relief from earthly suffering.

29. I see death as a relief from the burden of this life.

Unlike the landscape of Approach Acceptance, the emphasis is not so much on the joys to come in the next world, as it is on the end of suffering and pain in this world. Scripture readings, then, most helpfully focus on being sustained in the suffering of this time and having patience to wait until the time is "fulfilled" or completed. These readings can also center on the will of God that the sufferings of the present are the birth pains of another dimension being born in and through us.

I have found the idea of patient suffering as labor pains (see Romans 8: 18-25 in which the phrase "groaning in travail" comes straight from a birthing context) to be helpful in finding meaning in the pain. Meaningless pain is extremely difficult to bear but hoping that the pain leads to something better can make it more manageable and bearable.

The same method was used to find appropriate hymns as in previous chapters. I have deduced these themes from the statements of this landscape: Death is a relief from suffering, life is a burden, death will bring an end to all troubles and death is an escape from a terrible world.

As in the Approach Acceptance landscape, this is a way of conceiving of death that is very much present and nurtured in traditional Christian thought, ritual and hymnody.

SCRIPTURES
Deuteronomy 32: 10-14
Ps. 3
Ps.4
Ps. 5: 1-3,7-8,11-12
Ps. 6
Ps. 9:18
Ps. 10: 1,10-12,14,17-18
Ps. 12: 6
Ps. 13
Ps. 16. 1-2, 5-11
Ps. 17: 1-8
Ps. 18: 1-6, 31-33
Ps. 20: 1-5
Ps. 23
Ps. 25: 1-7, 16-22
Ps. 26: 1-3
Ps. 27: 1, 3-5, 7-9-, 13-14
Ps. 28: 1-2, 6-9

Ps. 30: 8-12
Ps. 31: 1-5, 9-10, 21-23
Ps. 32: 6-11
Ps. 33: 20-22
Ps. 34: 4-10
Ps. 37: 39-40
Ps. 39: 4-6, 12-13
Ps. 40: 1-3b, 11-17
Ps. 42
Ps. 43: 5
Ps. 46
Ps. 51: 1-2, 10-12
Ps. 54: 1-2
Ps. 55: 1-2b, 16-18, 22
Ps. 56: 8-13
Ps. 57: 1-3, 7-11
Ps. 59: 16-17
Ps. 61: 1-5
Ps. 62: 1-2, 5-8
Ps. 63 1-8
Ps. 66: 16-20
Ps. 69: 1-3, 13-18
Ps. 70
Ps. 71: 1-3
Ps. 73: 21-26
Ps. 77
Ps. 84
Ps. 86: 1-13
Ps. 88
Ps. 90: 1-6, 13-17
Ps. 91
Ps. 102
Ps. 103
Ps. 104
Ps. 118: 5-9
Ps. 119: 153-160

Ps. 121
Ps. 126
Ps. 130
Ps. 131
Ps. 138: 7-8
Ps. 139: 1-12
Ps. 142: 1-6b
Ps. 143: 1-2, 7-8
John 14
John 15: 1-17
Romans 8: 18-25
Romans 8: 31, 35-39
Phil 3: 20-21
I Pet. 1: 3-5
Rev. 3: 20-21
Rev. 21: 1-7

Hymns

DEATH IS A RELIEF FROM SUFFERING

Abide With Me
Amazing Grace
Beams of Heaven as I Go
Because He Lives
Because the Lord Is My Shepherd
Bringing in the Sheaves
Christ Be Our Light
Close to Thee
Eye Has Not Seen
I Heard the Voice of Jesus Say
If God Is For Us
Jesus is all the World to me
Jesus, Healer of Wounded Souls
Jesus, Lead the Way
Jesus, Lover of My Soul
Leave it There
My Faith Looks Up to Thee
Nothing Between
On Jordan's Stormy Banks I Stand
Precious Lord, Take my Hand
Precious Name
Pues Si Vivimus (When We are Living)
Shepherd of My Heart
There's Within My Heart a Melody
Trust and Obey
Victory in Jesus
You Are Mine

LIFE IS A BURDEN

A Shelter in the Time of Storm
Blest Be the Lord
Come Lord Jesus
Come, O Thou Traveler Unknown
Daw-Kee, Aim-Tsi-Taw (Great Spirit, Now I Pray)
He Touched Me
How Can I Keep From Singing
I Am Goin' to Moan When the Spirit Says Moan
Lo, How a Rose E'er Blooming
More Love to Thee, O Christ
Nada Te Turbe/Nothing Can Trouble
Nobody Knows the Trouble I've Seen
O Star of Truth
Psalm 42 (As the Deer Longs)
Remember Your Love
Soldiers of Christ Arise
Song of the Exile
Stand By Me
Sweet Hour of Prayer
Take Up Thy Cross
To You, O Lord
We Are Climbing Jacob's Ladder
We'll Understand it Better By and By
Weary of All Trumpeting
Within Our Darkest Night

END OF ALL TROUBLES

Come Sunday
Come to me, O Weary Traveler
Holy Darkness
It Is Well With My Soul
O Mary Don't You Weep
Precious Lord
Roll Away the Stone
Shall We Gather at the River?
The Rock That Is Higher Than I
Turn Our Hearts
We Walk By Faith/In Times of Trouble

ESCAPE FROM TERRIBLE WORLD

By Gracious Power
Come To Me
Eye Has Not Seen
How Firm a Foundation
Jesus, Lover of My Soul
Jesus, Savior, Pilot Me
My Hope Is Built
Nearer My God to Thee
Precious Lord, Take My Hand
Stand up, Stand up for Jesus
Steal Away to Jesus

PRAYERS

Our pain is destroying
    Our personhood,
O God our strength;
    It is beyond
What we can bear
    And we need
You to help us
    Shoulder the burden.

Grant us relief
    From this piercing pain
That we might
    Find our final
Repose and rest
    In your arms.

Grant us your vision
    Of the span
Of our lives
    So we can
Wait patiently
    For the final hour.

Keep us from
    Utter despair
About your love
    For us
And strengthen our faith
    In a future
You have planned
    With you forever.
    Amen

It's been a long journey
    O Beckoning God.
The road has
    Often seemed longer
Than our energies
    And its end
Has been out of sight.

Give us faith
    That the goal
Of our journey
    Here is in sight;
Help us see
    The riches of eternity
Just around the next bend.

Remind us
    It is just one
Step at a time
    That leads us home.

The terrors that
    Have afflicted us
Will soon be
    Behind us,
And before us
    Will only be delight.

Focus our vision
    On the delight
That awaits us
    So the pain
Of this moment
    Becomes less relevant.

Lift us from suffering,
    Establish us in your peace

And bring us to the place
    Where you, yourself,
Will wipe away our tears
    And embrace us in love
Everlasting. **Amen**

Our life has become
    A burden to us
And to our families
    O merciful God.

We have borne
    More than we
Ever thought possible
    And have long since
Earned a respite
    For ourselves
And our loved ones.

Take us home.
    O Welcoming God;
Let us slough
    Off this mortal coil
And be dressed
    By you, personally,
In the raiment
    Of heaven.

Comfort our families
    With the sure knowledge
That we will
    Soon be
Relieved of suffering
    And clothed in splendor;
Remind them that
    This is what

We have desired
    And you have blessed
With the hope
    Of Abundant Life
Opened for us
    Through Jesus Christ our Lord,
In whose name we pray
Amen.

Our lives are long spent
    O God, our Refuge.
We have been
    Living on fumes
And borrowing
    From a future
In which we have
    Not invested.

Take us home,
    O God, our creator.
Lift us from
    The shadows of earth
And bring us
    Fully into the light
Of your eternity.

End our pain
    And bring down
The curtain on this
    Life of struggle
So we might
    Enjoy our lives
Again as you
    Have always intended.

Remind our families
    That our hope

Of being restored
    To complete health
Is based on your
    Healing eternity
And not on our
    Own understanding.

Give all of us
    A vision of our lives
Restored to full vitality
    That our fears
About the future
    Will be eased
And we will
    Be encouraged to let go
Of this painful life
    In order to receive
The life that is coming
    To us all. **Amen**.

This world, Lord of all,
    Has become a curse
And not a blessing
    As you have intended.

We are at the
    End of our rope;
We have exhausted
    Our resources
And extinguished
    All the joys
We once, here, enjoyed.

It's our desire
    To flee home
To you, O God
    And rest;

Grant us, our wish,
    In this hour
If it be your will
    O God of life.

Accompany us
    In the transition
From this life
    To the life to come
So we might
    Have the strength
To go all the way
    Into the fullness
Of your restoring presence.

Ease our fears,
    Pave the way
Home with thanksgiving
    That our coming
Into your presence
    May restore us
To the fullness
    Of life
And the abundance
    Of health. **Amen.**

Chapter Eight

The Variegated Landscape: All Over the Place

It has been helpful, for explanation purposes, to refer to patients as if they will only be in one landscape. The reality is far more complicated. The developers of the DAP-R realized this and noted that the way the different domains interact with each other for each person will be what makes each person's experience unique.

The questions involved become those of professional and experiential judgment and spiritual discernment. How much fear is there for those who proclaim to be in Approach Acceptance? Those who present themselves as neutral acceptors might also have a sense of looking forward to the next adventure. Those who are fearful, who are religiously observant, will have some of the traditional, probably Western, ideas of the afterlife and the purported joys of heaven.

And, of course, there will be times when our patients and their loved ones will change the landscape they are traveling through from day to day or moment to moment. Because there is such high internal consistency between the statements in each landscape I have selected a representative landmark statement from each domain and used it to understand where the individuals and their families are at that moment.

So, for me, just five statements help give me a rule of thumb that makes it unnecessary to formally use the DAP-R each time I visit. The five statements that I use are:

18." I have an intense fear of death" representing the Fear of Death landscape.

3. "I avoid death thoughts at all costs" representing the Death Avoidance landscape.

14. "Death is a natural aspect of life" representing the Neutral Acceptance landscape.

4. "I believe I will be in heaven after I die" representing the Approach Acceptance landscape.

5. "Death will bring an end to all my troubles" representing the Escape Acceptance landscape.

I do not inflict these statements on the patients or families but wait for a natural opening in the conversation to bring them up. This way it becomes a natural part of the conversation and not contrived. I do try to structure the conversation, many times, in order to ascertain where the patient and their loved ones are, but this is an art that requires subtlety and nuance so they do not feel like they are being treated as objects and analyzed.

If the conversation lags, I will use another statement, from what I have discovered is their main landscapes, to clarify what they are experiencing and help them to feel they are understood and not alone. Since the statements are so closely related, I have a high degree of certainty that the question is relevant and not "out of left field" for those involved.

I can remember one conversation I had in which a lady in her 90's looked out her window, after a period of silence in the conversation, and noted that the trees were losing all their leaves.

"The seasons are changing," was my response. She nodded. It was clear to me this conversation was not about the trees. I waited to see where she might be going with this.

"Death is a natural aspect of life," I finally offered.

She agreed saying that she had a long life and reminisced about all the people who had gone before her who she hoped were waiting for her "on the other side."

"You are looking forward to a reunion with your loved ones," was my response.

"Yes," she said. "It has been a long time since I have seen some of them and it is getting near my time to go home.

"Your season of change has come?"

She nodded and wistfully replied, "Just like the trees."

In this conversation I used statements from the landscape of Neutral Acceptance and Approach Acceptance to walk with her through the particular landmarks of her experience. My responses were spot on and helped her know she was understood and not alone.

I used to prepare the same scripture reading and sing the same hymns for each patient. But now, I try to choose a scripture reading that is applicable to their particular understanding of the lay of the land in which they are traveling. So, for example, if they are primarily approach acceptance with fear mixed in, I will sing "How Great Thou Art" and "I've Got Peace Like a River"—if they are Christian—and then sing a hymn such as "Be Not Afraid." If singing isn't one of your gifts, burning a CD is very cheap these days.

I will also use one reading from the scriptures relating to the joys of heaven and another one that provides comfort in the midst of fear and anxiety.

The goal, in all encounters, is to understand the landscape the patient and his/her family is traversing so they will experience greater satisfaction in their journey. To respond in a rote way to a patient is about as helpful as nodding understanding to a two year old who is blathering away about something that we have difficulty understanding. The two year old may actually feel that we are listening but an adult wll not!

Studies tell us that patients who have more encounters with chaplains and spiritual care personnel feel that their care has been better—regardless of its technical excellence—and are less litigious. They are also more likely to feel that they received good care and share that with others.

Patient satisfaction being a very important indicator of quality care makes it more likely that some kind of approach marrying data and narrative will be used to document the quality of care. I hope this small contribution toward that goal has been helpful.

ENDNOTES

CHAPTER ONE
1. Ernest Becker, *The Denial of Death* (New York, Free Press, 1973) 87.
2. Becker ix cf. *Being With Dying*: "Virtuous King Yudhistara (the son of Yama, the Lord of Death) is asked, "What is the most wondrous thing in the world?" And Yudhistara replies, "The most wondrous thing in the world is that all around us people can be dying and we don't believe it can happen to us" from the Hindu epic *Mahabharata* p. 6.
3. Ken Wilber, *No Boundary* (Boston, Shambhala, 2001): "Indeed, the mind-body split and attendant dualism is a fundamental perspective of Western civilization" p. 6.
4. Wilber 23-24
5. Henri Nouwen, *The Way of the Heart* (Harper One, 1991). 72.
6. Nouwen. 73.
7. Nouwen. 76.
8. Edwin H. Friedman, *Generation to Generation* (The Guilford Press, 1985) 25-26.
9. Joan Halifax, *Being With Dying* (Boston: Shambhala,2009) xv.xvi.
10. Halifax 54.

CHAPTER TWO
1. Robert Kastenbaum, *The Psychology of Death* (New York, Springer Publishing Company, 2000) 264.
2. Kastenbaum 264.
3. Kastenbaum 264.
4. Paul T. P. Wong, Gary T. Reker and Gina Gesser, "Death Attitude Profile-Revised: A Multidimensional Measure of Attitudes Toward Death," *Death Anxiety*

Handbook: Research Instrumentation and Application, ed. Robert A. Neimeyer (Washington D.C, Taylor and Francis, 1994) 121-146.
5. Wong et. al 54
6. Wong et al 128
7. Wong et. al 138
8. Wong et.al. 138.
9. Wong et al. 138.
10. Wong et.al..141.
11. *see* Drew Gilpin Faust *This Republic of Suffering* (New York, Knopf, 2008)

CHAPTER FIVE
1. *see* Sedonia Cahill: "The Ceremonial Circle" at.http://www.the-great-adventure.com/prayers_readings_practices/prayers_and_readings.html
2. For an account of the death of Buddha see: http://www.as.miami.edu/phi/bio/Buddha/death.htm.

BIBLIOGRAPHY

Batastini, Robert J. and Cymbala, Michael A. *Gather*. Eds. Chicago: Gia Publications, Inc. 1994.

Becker, Ernest. *The Denial of Death*. New York: Free Press, 1973.

Belletini, Mark L..Chair,. *Singing the Living Tradition.* Boston: The Unitarian Universalist Association, 1993.

Faust, Drew Gilpin. *This Republic of Suffering*. New York: Knopf, 2008.

Halifax, Joan. *Being With Dying*. Boston: Shambhala, 2009.

Kalina, Kathy. *Midwife for Souls: Spiritual Care for the Dying*. Boston: Pauline, 2007.

Kastenbaum, Robert. *The Psychology of Death*. New York: Springer Publishing, 2000.

Kessler, David. *The Needs of the Dying*. Harper: 2007.

Mouw, Richard J. and Noll, Mark A. *Wonderful Words of Life: Hymns in American Protestant History and Theology*. Grand Rapids: Eerdmans Publishing.2004.

Neimeyer, Robert A. *Death Anxiety Handbook: Research, Instrumentation, and Application* Wahsington, D.C.: Taylor & Francis, 1994.

Nouwen, Henri. *The Way of the Heart*. New York: HarperOne. 1991.

Oregon Catholic Press, Publisher. *Breaking Bread*. Portland: Oregon, 2010.

Peterson, John W. *Living Praise Hymna*l. Grand Rapids: Singspiration Music, 1981.

Remen, Rachel Naomi, *Kitchen Table Wisdom*. New York: Riverhead Books, 2006.

Roberts, Elizabeth and Amidon, Elias. *Life Prayers From Around the World*. New York: Harper Colilins. 1996.

Singh, Kathleen Dowling. *The Grace in Dying.* New York: HarperSanFransico. 1998.

Wilber, Ken. *No Boundary.* Boston: Shambhala. 2001.

Young, Carlton. ed. *The United Methodist Hymnal.* Nashville: The United Methodist Publishing House. 1989.

Young, Carlton. ed. *The United Methodist Hymnal.* Nashville: The United Methodist Publishing House. 1966.

www.ingramcontent.com/pod-product-compliance
Lightning Source LLC
Chambersburg PA
CBHW060810050426
42449CB00008B/1620